What Others Say About Doug Giles

"I think Doug Giles brings a sharp, humorous, bold and captivating style to ministry that strikes a chord with young people."

– Dr. R.C. Sproul

"There is NO way to describe Doug Giles adequately, so I won't even try. Suffice it to say there is NO ONE like him and I'm grateful for him!"

– Eric Metaxas

"Doug Giles speaks the truth ... he's a societal watchdog ... a funny bastard."

– Ted Nugent

"Doug Giles is a good man, and his bambinas are fearless. His girls Hannah and Regis Giles are indefatigable. I admire the Giles clan from afar."

– Dennis Miller

"Doug Giles must be some kind of a great guy if CNN wants to impugn him."

– Rush Limbaugh

Dedication

Way back in the mid-1990s I heard Rick Godwin preach on the imprecatory psalms. He called them, "Dirty Harry Prayers." That message forever changed how and what I pray. Thanks Rick!

Copyright 2021, Doug Giles, All Rights Reserved

No part of this book may be reproduced, stored in a retrieval system, or transmitted by any means without the written permission of the author.

Published by White Feather Press.
(www.whitefeatherpress.com)

ISBN 978-1-61808-207-7

Printed in the United States of America

Cover design by David Bugnon and mobopolis.com

Scriptures marked KJV are taken from the KING JAMES VERSION (KJV): KING JAMES VERSION, public domain.

Scriptures marked TM are taken from the THE MESSAGE: THE BIBLE IN CONTEMPORARY ENGLISH (TM): Scripture taken from THE MESSAGE: THE BIBLE IN CONTEMPORARY ENGLISH, copyright©1993, 1994, 1995, 1996, 2000, 2001, 2002. Used by permission of NavPress Publishing Group

Psalms of War

Prayers that Literally Kick Ass

By Doug Giles

Table of Contents

Introduction..
About the Art. ....
Chapter One: A Psalm of War Against Evil Leaders............1
Chapter Two: A Psalm of War Against those Who
Persecute the Godly 5
Chapter Three: A Psalm of War Against Liars...................9
Chapter Four: A Psalm of War Against the Violent 15
Chapter Five: A Psalm of War Against Evil Schemers ... 23
Chapter Six: A Psalm of War Against the Slanderous 29
Chapter Seven: A Psalm of War Against those
Who Hate the Righteous 33
Chapter Eight: A Psalm of War Against the Implacable . 39
Chapter Nine: A Psalm of War Against Idolaters 43
Chapter Ten: A Psalm of War Against those Who
Set Traps for the Righteous 49
Chapter Eleven: A Psalm of War Against those
Who Curse You 57
Chapter Twelve: A Psalm of War Against Death Wishers 65
Chapter Thirteen: A Psalm of War Against
the Destroyers 69
Chapter Fourteen: A Psalm of War Against those
Who Love Mischief... 73
Chapter Fifteen: A Psalm of War Against those
Who Long for Chaos.. 77
Chapter Sixteen: A Psalm of War Against
the Gossipers 83
Chapter Seventeen: A Psalm of War Against
those Who Ambush The Righteous 89
Chapter Eighteen: A Psalm of War Against those
Who Try to Ruin Your Name 95
Chapter Nineteen: A Psalm of War Against All
Enemies of God.. 99

Chapter Twenty: A Psalm of War Against those
Who Hate You Without Cause 105

Chapter Twenty One: A Psalm of War Against
those Who Want God To Forsake You 111

Chapter Twenty Two: A Psalm of War Against
Forces Fighting Against the Church 117

Chapter Twenty Three: A Psalm of War Against
Enemies Infiltrating the Body of Christ........................... 123

Chapter Twenty Four: A Psalm of War Against
those Who Exalt Themselves above God 129

Chapter Twenty Five: A Psalm of War Against
Anti-Christian Blowhards 135

Chapter Twenty Six: A Psalm of War Against those
Who Make Life a Living Hell 139

Chapter Twenty Seven : A Psalm of War Against
those Who Make Everything Suck................................... 145

Chapter Twenty Eight : A Psalm of War Against
those Who Lie about You... 153

Introduction

Dear Christian: What do you pray for in a country that's governed by anti-theistic godless idiots who dream about dispensing with God and all things holy, just and good?

In addition, say that the powers of darkness are on you like stink on a monkey: What do you pray and how do you pray those malevolent forces away, huh?

Also, what do you pray if the Church you're a part of needs a massive revival because it has blown off seriously following the Rebel from Galilee and has morphed into a PC-addled religious social club?

Finally, what do you pray and say to your cantankerous flesh, that hates God and opposes your noble pursuit of the Son of Man?

One thing's for certain: sappy, *now-I-lay-me-down-to-sleep "prayers"* ain't gonna cut it when waging war against the aforementioned. Oh, heck no.

King David faced pure evil, in its multifaceted forms, when he kicked up dust on this *terra firma* three thousand years ago. He faced foes such as... ...

- Evil nations that hated God and His people.

- Evil "people of God" who tried to ruin his life and attempted to murder him.

- Evil priests and kings within the House of God

- Evil bents from his carnal flesh that tempted him to forsake God and listen to his lower cortex monkey brain that's always in agreement with the Devil.

Yep, David said the enemy had been, "plowing furrows"

in his back (Psalm 129) as long as he could remember! But the cool thing about David is he didn't take the enemy's crap laying down. He didn't curl up in the fetal position and wet his big Jewish diaper. He fought back. Sometimes he fought back physically. He always, constantly, fought back spiritually via worship and prayer. And not just any kind of "prayer", mind you, but a specific kind of prayer that you don't hear much about any more in your typical Cheesy Feelgood PC Church even though the Bible is replete with them.

Theologians call these prayers of David, imprecatory prayers, or maledictions. They are prayers to pull out and pray when things get bad. As in real bad. Prayers you use when a nation's getting mucked up by degenerate priests or politicians, or when the enemy is crushing the people of God, or when your personal demons/flesh is out of control.

So, who in the Scripture volleyed these Holy Spirit inspired invectives toward evil people and places? Well, aside from David, it was guys like Moses, Joshua, Jeremiah, Ezekiel, Paul and uh . . . let's see . . . there was someone else. Oh. I remember . . . Jesus. Yep, the Prince of Peace prayed and declared some not-so-nice maledictions against a gaggle of corrupt critters who were a hindrance to life and truth on His planet. For instance, sweet and cuddly, seven pound, thirteen ounce, baby Jesus said the following later on in life ...

> *"Woe to you, scribes and Pharisees, hypocrites! For you build the tombs of the prophets and adorn the monuments of the righteous, and say, 'If we had been living in the days of our fathers, we would not have been partners with them in shedding the blood of the prophets.' So you testify against yourselves, that you are sons of those who murdered the prophets. Fill up, then, the measure of the guilt of your fathers. You serpents, you brood of vipers, how will you escape the sentence of hell?"*
>
> Matthew 23:29-33 (KJV)

Matter of fact, Christ is credited with saying all the various "Woes (imprecations)" in the Gospels. What's the matter? Did they not tell you that at your youth group? It's true. Google it.

King David, however, at least from a recorded standpoint, was the king of this type of incendiary intercession. This giant killer slayed more Goliaths in his prayers and songs than he ever did with a rock and slingshot. Oh, and by the way, Jesus said all those imprecations David dealt out were not the mad ramblings of a ticked off warrior poet but were actually inspired by the Holy Spirit in Matthew 22:43. Check it out. Also, the apostle Paul also echoed the same sentiments when he told Timothy …

"All Scripture is inspired by God and beneficial for teaching, for rebuke, for correction, for training in righteousness ... " 2Timothy 3:16 (That "all scripture" entails all the imprecations within Holy Writ. Hello.)

Now, what follows is a sample list, from the book of Psalms, regarding how David rolled in prayer. I bet you haven't heard these read, prayed or sang in church against our formidable enemies, have you? I didn't think so. It might be time to dust them off and offer 'em up if you're truly concerned about the state of Christ's Church and our nation.

Here's how I recommend "reading" the Psalms of War …

1. Go through the table of contents and pick a topic/chapter title that currently concerns you. For instance, if you are sick of sorry, godless, leaders ruining our nation, a great place to start praying would be, *Chapter One: A Psalm of War Against Evil Leaders*. In addition, say you're beyond beleaguered with watching calamitous rioters ruin our cities. A great chapter to launch some Dirty Harry prayers at the demons behind that bellicose behavior would be, *Chapter Fifteen: A Psalm of War Against Those Who Long For Chaos*.

David had many enemies in his prayer crosshairs that he launched these invectives towards. Some physical, some spiritual and some internal. Anything standing between him accomplishing God's will, on this planet, received a verbal hailstorm from the slingshot swinging shepherd. I've included 20+ different topics/targets David hit on for you, the reader, to pick and pray in light of what the Lord is leading you to jackhammer in your current local condition.

2. Read them out loud. Yep, read them out loud, at the enemy, and with passion, against the demonic foes of the Church, Family and State.

   Indeed, don't just half-heartedly read these Imprecatory Psalms aloud. Do it with gusto. Get ticked off and bark 'em at the enemy. These prayers saved David's backside from some gnarly garbage. Give them their proper respect/gravitas they deserve by reading them aloud, with holy emotion, like your butt's in a similar sling as David's was back when he penned them.

3. Get your hipster worship team to stop singing their heretical and sappy and soulish "praise and worship" songs and put these bad boys back into play. You do know that these Psalms are the Bible's original butt-kicking hymnal, correct? And, I'm assuming, you do also know that Paul, by inspiration of the Holy Spirit, commanded Christians, in Ephesians 5:19, to "(Speak) to one another in *psalms* and hymns and spiritual songs, singing and making melody with your hearts to the Lord ..." Did you catch the "psalms" part of that verse? That would include the *Psalms of War* entailed herein.

4. So, think of this book as not only a compendium of various imprecations to pray against heaven's ubiquitous foes, but also a funky little journal that you can scribble victory notes in after Christ clocks whatever/whomever is battering you and the Church. Imagine praying these prayers and journaling your victories in this book for just a five year time period! It'll be a veritable legacy book that your kids and grandkids will fight over once you take the big dirt nap. Plus it'll also encourage them, when you're dead and gone, to also kick butt and take names for that which is holy, just and good.

5. Finally, this book will do you no good if you do not *boldly* confess these texts as *your* promises, and The Church's promises, given to the Body of Christ by God, The Father, to wage war against the powers of darkness. As stated, there are 20+ different imprecatory prayers in this fiery tome that are aimed at specific demonic attacks. Keep this book handy so that when you too undergo Satanic assault you'll be able scan the table of contents for the perfect prayer against the hordes of hell.

Ergo, my brothers and sisters, fight the enemies of God and mankind with what the Holy Ghost preserved for all eternity for the Christian to use against Satan's devices namely, the imprecatory prayers. Or what I like to call, *The Psalms of War.*

Oh, one more thing. Squishy Christians will be quick to say we shouldn't pray these prayers against our enemies or wish ill on our adversaries. First off, I agree. The imprecatory psalms are not curses to be tossed around by aggrieved Christians who want God to waylay everyone who is not like them. Secondly, our battle, predominantly, is not against flesh and blood (Ephesians 6:10-12) but demonic hordes. That said, and it's unfortunate, but demonic forces work through physical sinners to execute their dirty deeds, correct? So, it's a given, in our usage of imprecatory psalms against the clear enemies of God, that there will be human collateral damage of certain people who have decided to follow Satan's will and way verses God's. Therefore, in our volleying of these invectives, our heart should seek the repentance of those, who like Paul sided with the Devil out of ignorance, while leaving room for the wrath of God because He alone knows who are truly the implacable and impenitent and who are in line for a holy butt whuppin' from heaven.

Doug Giles
Somewhere in Texas
October, 2021

About the Art

All of the artwork entailed in this book was painted by me. The biblical characters I've depicted are from my *Biblical Badass Series* of oil paintings. I did a short film about this series that can be seen at DougGiles.Art.

Most of the original pieces have been sold but we do have prints available in custom sizes ranging from small to extra large.

I hope you enjoy the art while you're being armed with these *Psalms of War.*

Unless marked otherwise, scripture quoted in this book is taken from the original King James Version of the Bible which was first published in 1611.

The King James Version (KJV) is an English translation of the Christian Bible for the Church of England, which was commissioned in 1604 and sponsored by King James VI.

The King James Version was first printed by Robert Baker and John Norton, who held the position of the Royal Printer. It was the third translation into the English language and was approved by the English Church authorities.

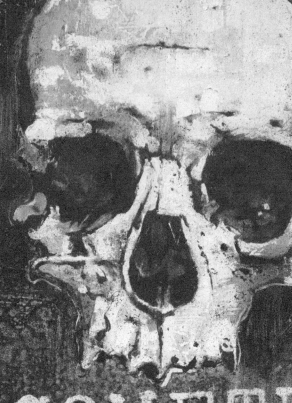

Chapter 1.
A Psalm of War Against Evil Leaders

A lot of people -- for many, many serious reasons -- are wringing their hands nowadays over the glide path our nation is tooling down thanks to the Marxist morons inside the Beltway.

Yep, at this writing, our current bevy of "elected" leaders care for that which is holy, just, and good about as much as badger cares what a prairie dog feels when he's chewing on its carotid artery.

I've personally seen and heard many Christians buy into this handwringing over the state of our union and I have wondered aloud, "Why don't you, dear Christian, cease to sweat these godless leaders and pray that God either convert them or take them out?"

Here in Psalm 2, David's not sweating a culture's smack-talking against God. He's not curled up in the fetal position, sucking his thumb, and wetting his pants over their godless and goofy plots to be free of God and cut loose from His law.

Matter of fact, David's reaction is just the opposite of what most doom-n-gloom Christians are boo-hooing about during these days of declension.

Indeed, David states that when rebel-kings start crap-talking God and attempt to dispense with His decrees -- that God mocks them. Yep, Jehovah's amused at these presumptive idiots who wish to lead a nation without giving God honor by adhering to His way.

And He doesn't just laugh, as you're about to see, He gets ticked off and that's bad news bears for the fools attempting to cast loose from God's gracious moorings.

Ergo, dear Christian, instead of chewing your fingernails down to the nub and buying the fear that saddles the faithless, why don't you pray out loud Psalm 2 that David prayed and penned many moons ago?

PSALM 2 (KJV)

1 Why do the heathen rage, and the people imagine a vain thing?

2 The kings of the earth set themselves, and the rulers take counsel together, against the Lord, and against his anointed, saying,

3 Let us break their bands asunder, and cast away their cords from us.

4 He that sitteth in the heavens shall laugh: the Lord shall have them in derision.

5 Then shall he speak unto them in his wrath, and vex them in his sore displeasure.

Psalms of War

6 Yet have I set my king upon my holy hill of Zion.

7 I will declare the decree: the Lord hath said unto me, Thou art my Son; this day have I begotten thee.

8 Ask of me, and I shall give thee the heathen for thine inheritance, and the uttermost parts of the earth for thy possession.

9 Thou shalt break them with a rod of iron; thou shalt dash them in pieces like a potter's vessel.

Chapter 2
A Psalm of War Against those Who Persecute the Godly

I have an old King James Bible with an intro to Psalm 3 that says King David penned this poem when he was fleeing from his son Absalom who was trying to kill him.

The familial hell in David's household was brought on by David himself. His adultery with Bathsheba and his successful plan to cover up his liaison with his new lady by having her husband murdered equated a holy butt whuppin' from God (2 Sam.12:11) in the form of massive family problems.

Most Christians, if they screwed up so royally like David did, would probably be beset with guilt and condemnation for the rest of their days. Indeed, el Diablowould work them over with Linda Ronstadt's lyrics, "You're no good. You're no good. You're no good. Baby, you're no good" and most Christians would buy that skubalon and ask for seconds.

David, on the other hand, truly knew God and thus knew His grace and therefore continued as God's special boy full of faith and boldness even after he had blown it badly.

Question: Have you to screwed up royally like David? If yes, don't throw away your confidence in God. David didn't and you shouldn't. Look how David rolled after getting rolled by his bedeviled demonic desires. It's pretty impressive how he bounced back from those heinous sins with his forceful faith intact.

Psalm 3 is the perfect psalm to pray and sing when you have enemies past counting who hope that God abandons you. David let this prayer rip against the devils hellbent on his demise and so should you. Don't be bashful, be bold and now pray this to God and ask Him to slap the faces and break the teeth of the powers of darkness and their minions who do their dirty work against you.

PSALM 3 (KJV)

1 Lord, how are they increased that trouble me! many are they that rise up against me.

2 Many there be which say of my soul, There is no help for him in God. Selah.

3 But thou, O Lord, art a shield for me; my glory, and the lifter up of mine head.

4 I cried unto the Lord with my voice, and he heard me out of his holy hill. Selah.

5 I laid me down and slept; I awaked; for the Lord sustained me.

6 I will not be afraid of ten thousands of people, that have set themselves against me round about.

Psalms of War

7 Arise, O Lord; save me, O my God: for thou hast smitten all mine enemies upon the cheek bone; thou hast broken the teeth of the ungodly.

8 Salvation belongeth unto the Lord: thy blessing is upon thy people. Selah.

Chapter 3
A Psalm of War Against Liars

Whoever said that life would be a lite beer commercial, 24/7/365, was full of more crap than a West Texas stockyard. In addition, if you came to Christ to have a carefree, no conflict existence, then you, my friend, are nuttier than a squirrel turd.

Real-life and true Christianity does not extricate one from chaos, spiritual warfare, and just common everyday bunkum. Matter of fact, closing in with Christ actually guarantees you're going to have more hell on earth than the godless clods experience because you, my friend, represent Satan's demise and he's not thrilled about that.

Therefore, buckle up, buttercup. It's going to get rougher than grandma's breath before it gets better.

One of the ways Satan tries to crush or sully the saints is via the satanic slinging of what is known in the Latin as, stercore tauri. Or what we call it down here in Texas, bullcrap.

If Satan's anything, he's a smack-talker and he wields his poisonous tongue quite often against God's elect. Satan, and the idiots he utilizes -- which extends to daft Christians as well -- employ lies hype, and spin to discourage and thereby neutralize the Christians' effectiveness.

Never fear, however! Psalm 5:1-12 is here!

Yes, child of God, if you have demons and dolts spewing their poison gas about you, setting spiritual IEDs in your path, whose throat is a veritable open grave of garbage, then launch Psalm 5:1-12 in their direction and watch what God does to them.

In addition, this is a great prayer to pray against those who persecute the people of God from their governmental positions.

Enjoy and share it with those who're being lied about.

Now commence crushing demons.

Psalms of War

Psalm 5:1-12 (KJV)

1 Give ear to my words, O Lord, consider my meditation.

2 Hearken unto the voice of my cry, my King, and my God: for unto thee will I pray.

3 My voice shalt thou hear in the morning, O Lord; in the morning will I direct my prayer unto thee, and will look up.

4 For thou art not a God that hath pleasure in wickedness: neither shall evil dwell with thee.

5 The foolish shall not stand in thy sight: thou hatest all workers of iniquity.

6 Thou shalt destroy them that speak leasing: the Lord will abhor the bloody and deceitful man.

7 But as for me, I will come into thy house in the multitude of thy mercy: and in thy fear will I worship toward thy holy temple.

8 Lead me, O Lord, in thy righteousness because of mine enemies; make thy way straight before my face.

9 For there is no faithfulness in their mouth; their inward part is very wickedness; their throat is an open sepulchre; they flatter with their tongue.

10 Destroy thou them, O God; let them fall by their own counsels; cast them out in the multitude of their transgressions; for they have rebelled against thee.

11 But let all those that put their trust in thee rejoice: let them ever shout for joy, because thou defendest them: let them also that love thy name be joyful in thee.

12 For thou, Lord, wilt bless the righteous; with favour wilt thou compass him as with a shield.

Chapter 4
A Psalm of War Against the Violent

When one conjures up in their whirring tin brain nowadays what it means to be a good "Christian", who has a "personal relationship with Jesus Christ", one imagines …

1. A nice old man who wears a cardigan, lives comfortably, watches Mike Huckabee, and says, "God bless you" every time you sneeze.

2. Some elderly lady who clutches her pearls and says, "Oh, my!" when she sees a Kim Kardashian butt pic on Watters World via the Fox News Channel.

3. A big, teenaged, frizzy-haired, barefooted girl who dons a "We The Kingdom" t-Shirt, wears stretch pants, dances with a scarf during worship, and

thinks holy water is a real thing.

4. A male hipster dandy who loves skinny jeans, sports a man bag and quotes more aphorisms during the student Bible study at Starbucks than would an over-medicated Joel Osteen on a three-day Mountain Dew bender.

Suffice to say, in the American evangelical milieu, being a Christian and having a "close walk with God" is a very comfortable thing but it was not so for King David.

Being "a man after God's own heart" cost David a pound of flesh.

It meant David was on Satan's Most Wanted list of folks Lucifer would love to obliterate.

Awww. What's the matter?

Did they not tell you that in your "youth group?"

Here's the reality, Ms. Kumbaya: to truly follow The Rebel from Galilee, to live as He lived, and say what He said, in this adulterous and perverted generation will land you in scalding hot water with all that is wicked.

David had to run for dear life at times from fierce "lions" who wanted to tear him to shreds and David wasn't speaking "spiritually", but literally. They truly wanted him dead because in his live, fire-breathing form, David was a wrecking crane to their idols and their evil machinations.

Psalm 7 shows David in the throes of a serious altercation and how he sang and prayed to God for deliverance. If you're also in such a fray I suggest the following: Lather. Rinse. And repeat what David said here with faith and force and watch God vanquish your foes.

Psalms of War

P**SALM** 7 (KJV)

1 O Lord my God, in thee do I put my trust: save me from all them that persecute me, and deliver me:

2 Lest he tear my soul like a lion, rending it in pieces, while there is none to deliver.

3 O Lord my God, If I have done this; if there be iniquity in my hands;

4 If I have rewarded evil unto him that was at peace with me; (yea, I have delivered him that without cause is mine enemy:)

5 Let the enemy persecute my soul, and take it; yea, let him tread down my life upon the earth, and lay mine honour in the dust. Selah.

6 Arise, O Lord, in thine anger, lift up thyself because of the rage of mine enemies: and awake for me to the judgment that thou hast commanded.

7 So shall the congregation of the people compass thee about: for their sakes therefore return thou on high.

8 The Lord shall judge the people: judge me, O Lord, according to my righteousness, and according to mine integrity that is in me.

9 Oh let the wickedness of the wicked come to an end; but establish the just: for the righteous God trieth the hearts and reins.

10 My defence is of God, which saveth the upright in heart.

11 God judgeth the righteous, and God is angry with the wicked every day.

12 If he turn not, he will whet his sword; he hath bent his bow, and made it ready.

13 He hath also prepared for him the instruments of death; he ordaineth his arrows against the persecutors.

14 Behold, he travaileth with iniquity, and hath conceived mischief, and brought forth falsehood.

15 He made a pit, and digged it, and is fallen into the ditch which he made.

16 His mischief shall return upon his own head, and his violent dealing shall come down upon his own pate.

17 I will praise the Lord according to his righteousness: and will sing praise to the name of the Lord most high.

Psalms of War

Chapter Five: A Psalm of War Against Evil Schemers

Have you ever looked at clearly wicked, impenitent, people and leaders and think, "Why the heck are they prospering and their wretched schemes succeeding?"

In the meantime, in-between time, folks that are trying to do right, obey God, and influence society with the gracious biblical worldview, are getting kicked by culture like a stuck door at Chuck Norris's house.

Yep, in today's jacked-up world, evil gets the green light and Christianity gets cancelled. It seems whacked and highly "unfair" that the aforementioned appears to be the case.

One would almost think that there is no God, or if there is one, He sure doesn't give one flibbertigibbet about what's going down on this third rock from the sun because the spawns of Satan seem to be winning and God's people are getting the shiitake mushrooms stomped out of them.

One thing for the Christian to consider before they get all

gloomy and begin to make Van Gogh look like a rodeo clown is this: just because God isn't visibly kicking the wicked's backside, doesn't mean an ass-whuppin' is not coming.

David dealt with this dilemma in Psalm 10. The wicked during his day plotted against him and Israel. They taunted Jehovah. They defied the people of God. They hunted down the righteous. They scorned God and, seemingly, they were getting away with it. Yep, they were cocksure they would never be held accountable for their hellish actions. But that's where the malicious were wrong. As in, dead wrong.

Look at what David prayed at these hounds from hell. Pay particular attention to verses fifteen and sixteen.

Remember to pray Psalm 10 the next time you begin to think the wicked will get away with their wickedness and the righteous are doomed to be Satan's doormat.

Psalm 10 (KJV)

1 Why standest thou afar off, O Lord? why hidest thou thyself in times of trouble?

2 The wicked in his pride doth persecute the poor: let them be taken in the devices that they have imagined.

3 For the wicked boasteth of his heart's desire, and blesseth the covetous, whom the Lord abhorreth.

4 The wicked, through the pride of his countenance, will not seek after God: God is not in all his thoughts.

5 His ways are always grievous; thy judgments are far above out of his sight: as for all his enemies, he puffeth at them.

6 He hath said in his heart, I shall not be moved: for I shall never be in adversity.

7 His mouth is full of cursing and deceit and fraud:

Psalms of War

under his tongue is mischief and vanity.

8 He sitteth in the lurking places of the villages: in the secret places doth he murder the innocent: his eyes are privily set against the poor.

9 He lieth in wait secretly as a lion in his den: he lieth in wait to catch the poor: he doth catch the poor, when he draweth him into his net.

10 He croucheth, and humbleth himself, that the poor may fall by his strong ones.

11 He hath said in his heart, God hath forgotten: he hideth his face; he will never see it.

12 Arise, O Lord; O God, lift up thine hand: forget not the humble.

13 Wherefore doth the wicked contemn God? he hath said in his heart, Thou wilt not require it.

14 Thou hast seen it; for thou beholdest mischief and spite, to requite it with thy hand: the poor committeth himself unto thee; thou art the helper of the fatherless.

15 Break thou the arm of the wicked and the evil man: seek out his wickedness till thou find none.

16 The Lord is King for ever and ever: the heathen are perished out of his land.

17 Lord, thou hast heard the desire of the humble: thou wilt prepare their heart, thou wilt cause thine ear to hear:

18 To judge the fatherless and the oppressed, that the man of the earth may no more oppress.

Chapter Six: A Psalm of War Against the Slanderous

In our prissy current culture of wokeness, everyone is scared to death of getting on the wrong side of the pissants who make up the self-appointed Thought Police.

There're massive companies raking in millions helping people clean up old tweets, remove bad reviews about their person, or their goods, services, or merchandise.

People are terrified about being lied about or ... gasp ... possibly unliked on Google or social media.

David dealt with similar twaddle when he toured this blue marble. David, however, didn't have ReputationDefender.com to go to bat for him and clear up any hogwash his haters were spewing about him.

Yep, the giant killer didn't have a killer giant company to set the record straight and defend David's life before the fickle plebes who made up ancient Israel.

Poor David. What's a shepherd boy to do?

Well, what David lacked in the natural realm to contend against untoward foes, he made up in spades in the supernatural realm having The Defender running interference for him.

Indeed, David called upon God, not Mark Zuckerberg, to sort out those who sought to sully his name.

If you're currently being lied about, or dasypygals are haranguing you by bringing up some past blunder, my advice would be to pull a Psalm 17 prayer out and shoot it heavenward and ask God to fight for you while you chill and take a big nap at rest in His love.

PSALM 17 (KJV)

1 Hear a just cause, O Lord, give heed to my cry;
Give ear to my prayer, which is not from deceitful lips.

2 Let my judgment come forth from Your presence;
Let Your eyes look with equity.

3 You have tried my heart;
You have visited *me* by night;
You have tested me and You find nothing;
I have purposed that my mouth will not transgress.

4 As for the deeds of men, by the word of Your lips
I have kept from the paths of the violent.

5 My steps have held fast to Your paths.
My feet have not slipped.

6 I have called upon You, for You will answer me, O God; Incline Your ear to me, hear my speech.

7 Wondrously show Your lovingkindness,
O Savior of those who take refuge at Your right hand

Psalms of War

From those who rise up *against them*.

8 Keep me as the apple of the eye;
Hide me in the shadow of Your wings

9 From the wicked who despoil me,
My deadly enemies who surround me.

10 They have closed their unfeeling *heart*,
With their mouth they speak proudly.

11 They have now surrounded us in our steps;
They set their eyes to cast *us* down to the ground.

12 He is like a lion that is eager to tear,
And as a young lion lurking in hiding places.

13 Arise, O Lord, confront him, bring him low;
Deliver my soul from the wicked with Your sword,

14 From men with Your hand, O Lord,
From men of the world, whose portion is in *this* life,
And whose belly You fill with Your treasure;
They are satisfied with children,
And leave their abundance to their babes.

15 As for me, I shall behold Your face in righteousness;
I will be satisfied with Your likeness when I awake.

Chapter Seven: A Psalm of War Against those Who Hate the Righteous

If you're worth your salt, then you're going to be attacked more viciously than a case of Twinkies would be at a Rosie O'Donnell plus-sized slumber party.

I know they didn't tell you that at Leitaphart Community Church, but it is true. Jesus said, "If they hated me, they're going to hate you." And you would've known that if you had read your bible. Anyway ...

David was no stranger to hatred.

If the shepherd boy was around today slinging stones, beheading giants, and singing epic songs that literally exorcise devils from peoples' persons, he would be as ardently loved and vehemently loathed as he was 3,000 years ago.

Dealing with such a dichotomy of love and wrath can scramble your eggs.

It can make it difficult to know who to turn to for soul support.

Who the heck can you trust?

The "people of God," throughout David's life, were a main source of persecution. In other words, David ain't gonna get any solace unbearing his heavy burdens at the men's group meeting because most of those bastards hated him, were untrustworthy, and were longing for his demise.

Sometimes, oft times, and I know this isn't what Oprah would say, you the Christian, have to go at it alone with God. Some people think the aforementioned is so sad. I think it's so cool. Isn't that what Christianity is all about, knowing God and trusting Him and Him alone?

David trusted God and lifted up his soul to Him, at the exclusion of others, and asked the Lord, and Him alone, to not let his enemies get the upper hand and to not let him be ashamed.

Meditate on those first two verses in Psalm 25 and then enjoy the rest of this substantial song.

Psalm 25 (KJV)

1 Unto thee, O Lord, do I lift up my soul.

2 O my God, I trust in thee: let me not be ashamed, let not mine enemies triumph over me.

3 Yea, let none that wait on thee be ashamed: let them be ashamed which transgress without cause.

4 Shew me thy ways, O Lord; teach me thy paths.

5 Lead me in thy truth, and teach me: for thou art the

Psalms of War

God of my salvation; on thee do I wait all the day.

6 Remember, O Lord, thy tender mercies and thy lovingkindnesses; for they have been ever of old.

7 Remember not the sins of my youth, nor my transgressions: according to thy mercy remember thou me for thy goodness' sake, O Lord.

8 Good and upright is the Lord: therefore will he teach sinners in the way.

9 The meek will he guide in judgment: and the meek will he teach his way.

10 All the paths of the Lord are mercy and truth unto such as keep his covenant and his testimonies.

11 For thy name's sake, O Lord, pardon mine iniquity; for it is great.

12 What man is he that feareth the Lord? him shall he teach in the way that he shall choose.

13 His soul shall dwell at ease; and his seed shall inherit the earth.

14 The secret of the Lord is with them that fear him; and he will shew them his covenant.

15 Mine eyes are ever toward the Lord; for he shall pluck my feet out of the net.

16 Turn thee unto me, and have mercy upon me; for I am desolate and afflicted.

17 The troubles of my heart are enlarged: O bring thou me out of my distresses.

18 Look upon mine affliction and my pain; and forgive all my sins.

19 Consider mine enemies; for they are many; and they hate me with cruel hatred.

20 O keep my soul, and deliver me: let me not be ashamed; for I put my trust in thee.

21 Let integrity and uprightness preserve me; for I wait on thee.

22 Redeem Israel, O God, out of all his troubles.

Psalms of War

Chapter Eight: A Psalm of War Against the Implacable

In the squishy, nicer-than-Christ-churches, Jesus has nary a peep bad to say about mankind. Yep, Jesus is just an altruistic celestial sweetie-pie, whom the wicked can just trounce, blaspheme, and hee-haw at with zero repercussions whatsoever.

If you think I'm full of specious doo, take this test. Next time you go to a funeral of a friend or family member who did not give a flying' rat's backside about God, His Son, or His word, pay attention to what the minister says because I'll bet you a hundred bucks that Mr. Judas Priest placed him in Beulah Land eating ice cream with Jesus upon expiration.

We have all seen it.

Some notorious sinner who never repented, who hated God and His people, who ran with the Devil, a veritable full-time employee for evil, who spent many moons in Satan's workshop all the sudden, when they breathe their last ... Poof! ... they supposedly get sanctified by the grave, via the apostate pastor, during the eulogy.

David, via the inspiration of the Holy Spirit, begged to differ.

In Psalm 28, David said God's going to tear down the wicked and not build them up. Check out verse five if you don't believe me.

What a sober Psalm.

PSALM 28 (KJV)

1 Unto thee will I cry, O Lord my rock; be not silent to me: lest, if thou be silent to me, I become like them that go down into the pit.

2 Hear the voice of my supplications, when I cry unto thee, when I lift up my hands toward thy holy oracle.

3 Draw me not away with the wicked, and with the workers of iniquity, which speak peace to their neighbours, but mischief is in their hearts.

4 Give them according to their deeds, and according to the wickedness of their endeavours: give them after the work of their hands; render to them their desert.

5 Because they regard not the works of the Lord, nor the operation of his hands, he shall destroy them, and not build them up.

6 Blessed be the Lord, because he hath heard the voice of my supplications.

Psalms of War

7 The Lord is my strength and my shield; my heart trusted in him, and I am helped: therefore my heart greatly rejoiceth; and with my song will I praise him.

8 The Lord is their strength, and he is the saving strength of his anointed.

9 Save thy people, and bless thine inheritance: feed them also, and lift them up for ever.

Chapter Nine: A Psalm of War Against Idolaters

If you're a warrior in God's kingdom, and not some lukewarm, vomitous, blah blah blah, mediocre Christian, then you're under assault by the powers of darkness.

Sometimes it's way obvious.

For instance, you know you're under attack when your wife, during menopause, spawns enough personalities to form her own softball team.

In addition, ladies, you know your marriage is under siege when your grey-headed husband suddenly dyes his hair jet black, takes shirtless selfie pics post-workout, and spends six hours a day posting said pics to Facebook. You just know there's a Jezebel somewhere in that fetid mix.

Whether it's a temptation to eat three chicken fried steaks during lunch, watch midget porn, hold grudges for decades, drink a bottle of scotch for breakfast, believe anything AOC says, vote for Biden in 2024, or covet your neighbor's bass boat, a Christian worth a plug nickel knows that Satan has obvious multifaceted wares to woo us off the way to the Celestial City.

What's more unnerving to me are the slicker devices el Diablo wields our way to take us off the battlefield. These attacks are more subtle than the overt sex and money temptations and fall into stealth mode.

The Psalmist, here in Psalm 31, is freaking out over hidden traps and pernicious plots regarding how to ruin him for good. In other words, David's in deep yogurt because of his deep devotion to Jehovah. Ergo, in this song, the psalmist unleashes an imprecation of Divine intervention that all holy warriors should put on their shortlist of prayers against the unseen conspiracies that you just know Satan is setting for the totally committed.

PSALM 31 (KJV)

1 In thee, O Lord, do I put my trust; let me never be ashamed: deliver me in thy righteousness.

2 Bow down thine ear to me; deliver me speedily: be thou my strong rock, for an house of defence to save me.

3 For thou art my rock and my fortress; therefore for thy name's sake lead me, and guide me.

4 Pull me out of the net that they have laid privily for me: for thou art my strength

5 Into thine hand I commit my spirit: thou hast redeemed me, O Lord God of truth

6 I have hated them that regard lying vanities: but I

Psalms of War

trust in the Lord.

7 I will be glad and rejoice in thy mercy: for thou hast considered my trouble; thou hast known my soul in adversities;

8 And hast not shut me up into the hand of the enemy: thou hast set my feet in a large room.

9 Have mercy upon me, O Lord, for I am in trouble: mine eye is consumed with grief, yea, my soul and my belly.

10 For my life is spent with grief, and my years with sighing: my strength faileth because of mine iniquity, and my bones are consumed.

11 I was a reproach among all mine enemies, but especially among my neighbours, and a fear to mine acquaintance: they that did see me without fled from me.

12 I am forgotten as a dead man out of mind: I am like a broken vessel.

13 For I have heard the slander of many: fear was on every side: while they took counsel together against me, they devised to take away my life.

14 But I trusted in thee, O Lord: I said, Thou art my God.

15 My times are in thy hand: deliver me from the hand of mine enemies, and from them that persecute me.

16 Make thy face to shine upon thy servant: save me for thy mercies' sake.

17 Let me not be ashamed, O Lord; for I have called upon thee: let the wicked be ashamed, and let them be silent in the grave.

18 Let the lying lips be put to silence; which speak

grievous things proudly and contemptuously against the righteous.

19 Oh how great is thy goodness, which thou hast laid up for them that fear thee; which thou hast wrought for them that trust in thee before the sons of men!

20 Thou shalt hide them in the secret of thy presence from the pride of man: thou shalt keep them secretly in a pavilion from the strife of tongues.

21 Blessed be the Lord: for he hath shewed me his marvellous kindness in a strong city.

22 For I said in my haste, I am cut off from before thine eyes: nevertheless thou heardest the voice of my supplications when I cried unto thee.

23 O love the Lord, all ye his saints: for the Lord preserveth the faithful, and plentifully rewardeth the proud doer.

24 Be of good courage, and he shall strengthen your heart, all ye that hope in the Lord.

Psalms of War

Chapter Ten: A Psalm of War Against those Who Set Traps for the Righteous

My wife and I have two beautiful daughters. Both of them are on-fire warrior chicks for Christ. It's an epic thing to behold. It's hard to pick a favorite daughter because they're both so great.

That said, it's hard to pick a favorite Psalm. I love 'em all and they all were inspired by the Holy Ghost so, hello, I'd better like them equally.

With that qualifier out of the way, I must confess a special affinity for Psalm 35.

David was lit when he wrote this raucous song.

Yep, David wasn't playing like a nice little Jewish boy

penned this poem.

Pay particular attention to the way he's addressing God. It's rather stunning. Some would say it is almost presumptuous and rude. Genteel Christians would never be as bold as David was in his requests of the Father.

Thank God David wasn't wussified in his approach to God when David was in deep weeds.

Thank God David wasn't some prissy evangelical who had "learned to pray" from some other prissy evangelical.

What you have here in Psalm 35 is an unvarnished holy invective from a ticked-off warrior poet of which the Trinity said to themselves, "Y'know … that was awesome. Let's preserve that in Sacred Writ for all eternity so that tepid and scared little Christians can see how a real man of God should pray."

One last thing. Pray this prayer out loud, with passion, during your youth group, and take a video of the crowd's response. That should be interesting …

PSALM 35 (KJV)

1 Plead my cause, O Lord, with them that strive with me: fight against them that fight against me.

2 Take hold of shield and buckler, and stand up for mine help.

3 Draw out also the spear, and stop the way against them that persecute me: say unto my soul, I am thy salvation.

4 Let them be confounded and put to shame that seek after my soul: let them be turned back and brought to confusion that devise my hurt.

Psalms of War

5 Let them be as chaff before the wind: and let the angel of the Lord chase them.

6 Let their way be dark and slippery: and let the angel of the Lord persecute them.

7 For without cause have they hid for me their net in a pit, which without cause they have digged for my soul.

8 Let destruction come upon him at unawares; and let his net that he hath hid catch himself: into that very destruction let him fall.

9 And my soul shall be joyful in the Lord: it shall rejoice in his salvation.

10 All my bones shall say, Lord, who is like unto thee, which deliverest the poor from him that is too strong for him, yea, the poor and the needy from him that spoileth him?

11 False witnesses did rise up; they laid to my charge things that I knew not.

12 They rewarded me evil for good to the spoiling of my soul.

13 But as for me, when they were sick, my clothing was sackcloth: I humbled my soul with fasting; and my prayer returned into mine own bosom.

14 I behaved myself as though he had been my friend or brother: I bowed down heavily, as one that mourneth for his mother.

15 But in mine adversity they rejoiced, and gathered themselves together: yea, the abjects gathered themselves together against me, and I knew it not; they did tear me, and ceased not:

16 With hypocritical mockers in feasts, they gnashed upon me with their teeth.

17 Lord, how long wilt thou look on? rescue my soul from their destructions, my darling from the lions.

18 I will give thee thanks in the great congregation: I will praise thee among much people.

19 Let not them that are mine enemies wrongfully rejoice over me: neither let them wink with the eye that hate me without a cause.

20 For they speak not peace: but they devise deceitful matters against them that are quiet in the land.

21 Yea, they opened their mouth wide against me, and said, Aha, aha, our eye hath seen it.

22 This thou hast seen, O Lord: keep not silence: O Lord, be not far from me.

23 Stir up thyself, and awake to my judgment, even unto my cause, my God and my Lord.

24 Judge me, O Lord my God, according to thy righteousness; and let them not rejoice over me.

25 Let them not say in their hearts, Ah, so would we have it: let them not say, We have swallowed him up.

26 Let them be ashamed and brought to confusion together that rejoice at mine hurt: let them be clothed with shame and dishonour that magnify themselves against me.

27 Let them shout for joy, and be glad, that favour my righteous cause: yea, let them say continually, Let the Lord be magnified, which hath pleasure in the prosper-

Psalms of War

ity of his servant.

28 And my tongue shall speak of thy righteousness and of thy praise all the day long.

Chapter Eleven: A Psalm of War Against those Who Curse You

David's brothers hated him.
King Saul was jealous of David and tried to kill him twice.

A big chunk of the "people of God" followed King Saul and they too wanted David dead.

Welcome to church, eh?

The "People of God" were right up there with the Philistines as being a major pain in the butt for David.

Strange, isn't it?

Here's how it plays out in our day.

When one first gets saved everything seems so new and refreshing. Everyone's glad you got converted. You want to tell your story and people want to hear it. It's a wonderful little newlywed kind of feeling and then all of the sudden, once God gives you a vision, or you do something for God that other dullards cannot or would not do, then the sweet fellowship you enjoyed with the brethren evaporates like a pack of smokes at an AA meeting and gets replaced with envious "Christians" praying for your ruin.

Let me guess, they didn't tell you that in youth group?

David's intimacy and exploits for God drew out the worst in the people of God. Sure, some loved it, but make no mistake, others hated his guts because of his zeal and God's unique favor on his life.

David said these folks prayed for his ruin, tried to kidnap his soul, got a kick out of making him miserable, and booed and jeered him without mercy.

If you're going through similar gobbledegook from the "People of God" as David did in Psalm 40 then please take a gander at this psalm and pray it like the third monkey trying to get on Noah's Ark.

PSALM 40 (KJV)

1 I waited patiently for the Lord; and he inclined unto me, and heard my cry.

2 He brought me up also out of an horrible pit, out of the miry clay, and set my feet upon a rock, and established my goings.

3 And he hath put a new song in my mouth, even praise unto our God: many shall see it, and fear, and shall trust in the Lord.

4 Blessed is that man that maketh the Lord his trust,

Psalms of War

and respecteth not the proud, nor such as turn aside to lies.

5 Many, O Lord my God, are thy wonderful works which thou hast done, and thy thoughts which are to us-ward: they cannot be reckoned up in order unto thee: if I would declare and speak of them, they are more than can be numbered.

6 Sacrifice and offering thou didst not desire; mine ears hast thou opened: burnt offering and sin offering hast thou not required.

7 Then said I, Lo, I come: in the volume of the book it is written of me,

8 I delight to do thy will, O my God: yea, thy law is within my heart.

9 I have preached righteousness in the great congregation: lo, I have not refrained my lips, O Lord, thou knowest.

10 I have not hid thy righteousness within my heart; I have declared thy faithfulness and thy salvation: I have not concealed thy lovingkindness and thy truth from the great congregation.

11 Withhold not thou thy tender mercies from me, O Lord: let thy lovingkindness and thy truth continually preserve me.

12 For innumerable evils have compassed me about: mine iniquities have taken hold upon me, so that I am not able to look up; they are more than the hairs of mine head: therefore my heart faileth me.

13 Be pleased, O Lord, to deliver me: O Lord, make haste to help me.

14 Let them be ashamed and confounded together that seek after my soul to destroy it; let them be driven backward and put to shame that wish me evil.

15 Let them be desolate for a reward of their shame that say unto me, Aha, aha.

16 Let all those that seek thee rejoice and be glad in thee: let such as love thy salvation say continually, The Lord be magnified.

17 But I am poor and needy; yet the Lord thinketh upon me: thou art my help and my deliverer; make no tarrying, O my God.

Psalms of War

Chapter Twelve: A Psalm of War Against Death Wishers

As we're clearly seeing clipping through the Psalms of War, David's relationship with God was anything but puppy dogs, pixie dust, and candy canes. It was hectic, y'all.

David got tossed around in life more than a drunk midget would at a *Godsmack* concert.

Psalm 41:9 says this attack got personal, as in very personal. David got attacked by one of his best buddies. He was a true confidant, someone David wined and dined with at his house all the time, but who then decided to bite the hand that fed him.

David's own familiar amigo spoke the worst about him, placed bets on his demise, gossiped about him, whispered slanders around town about him, and formed a little cabal to plan misery for David.

Joy to the world, eh?

It sucks, but that's life in the real world.

If you're going through a similar woodchipper with a former confidant, well then … this Bud's for you.

Psalm 41 (KJV)

1 Blessed is he that considereth the poor: the Lord will deliver him in time of trouble.

2 The Lord will preserve him, and keep him alive; and he shall be blessed upon the earth: and thou wilt not deliver him unto the will of his enemies.

3 The Lord will strengthen him upon the bed of languishing: thou wilt make all his bed in his sickness.

4 I said, Lord, be merciful unto me: heal my soul; for I have sinned against thee.

5 Mine enemies speak evil of me, When shall he die, and his name perish?

6 And if he come to see me, he speaketh vanity: his heart gathereth iniquity to itself; when he goeth abroad, he telleth it.

7 All that hate me whisper together against me: against me do they devise my hurt.

8 An evil disease, say they, cleaveth fast unto him: and now that he lieth he shall rise up no more.

9 Yea, mine own familiar friend, in whom I trusted, which did eat of my bread, hath lifted up his heel against me.

10 But thou, O Lord, be merciful unto me, and raise me up, that I may requite them.

Psalms of War

11 By this I know that thou favourest me, because mine enemy doth not triumph over me.

12 And as for me, thou upholdest me in mine integrity, and settest me before thy face for ever.

13 Blessed be the Lord God of Israel from everlasting, and to everlasting. Amen, and Amen.

Chapter Thirteen: A Psalm of War Against the Destroyers

You know what's more obvious than the fact that Yoko Ono can't sing a flippin' lick?

It is this: On-fire Christians will be attacked by the world, the flesh, and the Devil.

If you've missed that point, at this juncture, in this book, then you, my dear reader, are definitely not the coldest beer in the cooler.

Given the fact that, in this world, you will have whacked crap come your way via satanic interference, in the form of bad government and bad religion (John.16:33) and fleshly bents, why do Christians still seem shocked when it happens?

The powers of darkness are supposed to assault the believer. You're their enemy. Hello! What do expect them to do, buy you a Slurpee?

David says here in Psalm 54 that he needs God to "save (him)" … from "strangers" and "oppressors" who were seeking "after his soul."

In other words, David's in a mell of a hess.

With a lot of Christians today, if they were in David's sandals, under that type of duress, the text would read that the strangers and the oppressors whupped the Christian's backside and Satan won that tussle.

Not so, here with David.

David says in the throes of a throw down with his enemies, God did the following to his adversaries …

1. God helped David.
2. God upheld David's soul.
3. God rewarded evil to David's enemies.
4. God cut David's attackers off.
5. God delivered David out of all his troubles.
6. And David got to see his enemies get fish-slapped by the mighty hand of God.

This should be our testimony when hell comes against us. Enjoy Psalm 54 and tuck this bad boy away in your prayer arsenal to use when "strangers" and "oppressors" attack your soul.

Psalm 54 (KJV)

1 Save me, O God, by thy name, and judge me by thy strength.

2 Hear my prayer, O God; give ear to the words of my mouth.

3 For strangers are risen up against me, and oppressors

Psalms of War

seek after my soul: they have not set God before them. Selah.

4 Behold, God is mine helper: the Lord is with them that uphold my soul.

5 He shall reward evil unto mine enemies: cut them off in thy truth.

6 I will freely sacrifice unto thee: I will praise thy name, O Lord; for it is good.

7 For he hath delivered me out of all trouble: and mine eye hath seen his desire upon mine enemies.

Chapter Fourteen: A Psalm of War Against those Who Love Mischief

It's expected that Satan should attack the Christian.

In addition, it ain't a shocker when anti-theistic hordes aren't mondo-jovial with the Christian implementation of the Biblical Worldview to broader society or our global evangelistic efforts to convert souls and disciple nations.

What does solidly gobsmack the saint is when a long-time "Christian" friend turns on you and betrays you.

Here, once again, in Psalm 55, David had his "friends" put daggers into his heart.

With friends like these, who needs enemies.

Doug Giles

Psalm 55 (KJV)

1 Give ear to my prayer, O God; and hide not thyself from my supplication.

2 Attend unto me, and hear me: I mourn in my complaint, and make a noise;

3 Because of the voice of the enemy, because of the oppression of the wicked: for they cast iniquity upon me, and in wrath they hate me.

4 My heart is sore pained within me: and the terrors of death are fallen upon me.

5 Fearfulness and trembling are come upon me, and horror hath overwhelmed me.

6 And I said, Oh that I had wings like a dove! for then would I fly away, and be at rest.

7 Lo, then would I wander far off, and remain in the wilderness. Selah.

8 I would hasten my escape from the windy storm and tempest.

9 Destroy, O Lord, and divide their tongues: for I have seen violence and strife in the city.

10 Day and night they go about it upon the walls thereof: mischief also and sorrow are in the midst of it.

11 Wickedness is in the midst thereof: deceit and guile depart not from her streets.

12 For it was not an enemy that reproached me; then I could have borne it: neither was it he that hated me that did magnify himself against me; then I would have hid myself from him:

13 But it was thou, a man mine equal, my guide, and

Psalms of War

mine acquaintance.

14 We took sweet counsel together, and walked unto the house of God in company.

15 Let death seize upon them, and let them go down quick into hell: for wickedness is in their dwellings, and among them.

16 As for me, I will call upon God; and the Lord shall save me.

17 Evening, and morning, and at noon, will I pray, and cry aloud: and he shall hear my voice.

18 He hath delivered my soul in peace from the battle that was against me: for there were many with me.

19 God shall hear, and afflict them, even he that abideth of old. Selah. Because they have no changes, therefore they fear not God.

20 He hath put forth his hands against such as be at peace with him: he hath broken his covenant.

21 The words of his mouth were smoother than butter, but war was in his heart: his words were softer than oil, yet were they drawn swords.

22 Cast thy burden upon the Lord, and he shall sustain thee: he shall never suffer the righteous to be moved.

23 But thou, O God, shalt bring them down into the pit of destruction: bloody and deceitful men shall not live out half their days; but I will trust in thee.

Chapter Fifteen: A Psalm of War Against those Who Long for Chaos

What's lost on a lot of readers of the various Psalms is that they are actual songs.

When David got assaulted by his ubiquitous enemies, instead of calling a 1-800 prayer line, he sang.

Weird, eh?

Most Christians when they're getting waylaid by the powers of darkness start whining or complaining, or they call their prayer partner, or if it's really bad they go to a counselor and blather on about their plight for the next seven and a half Olympics. Not so with David.

David sang praises to God in the midst of his storms. Yep, when the crap was hitting the fan here in Psalm 56 David sang his way out.

I think we ought to do that, namely praise God, first and foremost, when we're in the midst of a hellish firefight.

PSALM **56** (KJV)

1 Be merciful unto me, O God: for man would swallow me up; he fighting daily oppresseth me.

2 Mine enemies would daily swallow me up: for they be many that fight against me, O thou most High.

3 What time I am afraid, I will trust in thee.

4 In God I will praise his word, in God I have put my trust; I will not fear what flesh can do unto me.

5 Every day they wrest my words: all their thoughts are against me for evil.

6 They gather themselves together, they hide themselves, they mark my steps, when they wait for my soul.

7 Shall they escape by iniquity? in thine anger cast down the people, O God.

8 Thou tellest my wanderings: put thou my tears into thy bottle: are they not in thy book?

9 When I cry unto thee, then shall mine enemies turn back: this I know; for God is for me.

10 In God will I praise his word: in the Lord will I praise his word.

11 In God have I put my trust: I will not be afraid what

Psalms of War

man can do unto me.

12 Thy vows are upon me, O God: I will render praises unto thee.

13 For thou hast delivered my soul from death: wilt not thou deliver my feet from falling, that I may walk before God in the light of the living?

Chapter Sixteen: A Psalm of War Against the Gossipers

I don't know if you're noticing yet, but there is a bigger than Dallas difference between the way that David prayed and sang and the way your nicer-than-Christ pastor prays and sings.

A BIG difference.

David describes the demonic hordes that have set themselves against him in Psalm 58 as ...

1. Evil from the cradle.

2. Poisonous snakes.

So, what does the sweet Psalmist request of God to do regarding this bellicose bunch that's gang tackling Jesus' great-granddad?

Well, succinctly, David requests the following:

1. Break their teeth in their mouth.
2. Let them melt away.
3. Cut them in pieces.
4. Melt 'em like a snail.
5. Let them not see the sun.
6. Hit 'em with a tornado.

Can you imagine what damage Christians could do to Satan's devices if they just got a little more biblical in their bluster when they engaged in prayer and worship, as illustrated here?

Turn them into snail slime, Oh God.

Break their teeth, Lord!

Say that next time someone asks you to pray and see what happens.

PSALM 58 (KJV)

1 Do ye indeed speak righteousness, O congregation? do ye judge uprightly, O ye sons of men

2 Yea, in heart ye work wickedness; ye weigh the violence of your hands in the earth.

3 The wicked are estranged from the womb: they go astray as soon as they be born, speaking lies.

4 Their poison is like the poison of a serpent: they are like the deaf adder that stoppeth her ear;

5 Which will not hearken to the voice of charmers, charming never so wisely.

6 Break their teeth, O God, in their mouth: break out

Psalms of War

the great teeth of the young lions, O Lord.

7 Let them melt away as waters which run continually: when he bendeth his bow to shoot his arrows, let them be as cut in pieces.

8 As a snail which melteth, let every one of them pass away: like the untimely birth of a woman, that they may not see the sun.

9 Before your pots can feel the thorns, he shall take them away as with a whirlwind, both living, and in his wrath.

10 The righteous shall rejoice when he seeth the vengeance: he shall wash his feet in the blood of the wicked.

11 So that a man shall say, Verily there is a reward for the righteous: verily he is a God that judgeth in the earth.

Chapter Seventeen: A Psalm of War Against those Who Ambush the Righteous

Pastors nowadays refer to Jesus as one's "personal Savior".

How quaint, eh?

In Psalm 59, David, being the constantly in trouble child of God that he was, saw God not just as some amorphous "personal Savior" but referred to God as ...

1. Lord God of Hosts ("Hosts" means, "Angelic armies").
2. The God of my mercy.
3. O Lord our Shield.
4. The God who rules to the ends of the earth.
5. God of my defense.

Matter of fact, David had a litany of names and descriptions for the Shepherd of his soul throughout the Psalms. Check it out ...

Names of God in the Book of Psalms
The Lord – 1:2
God of my righteousness – 4:1
My King – 5:2
Oh Lord my God – 7:1
God of my salvation – 18:46
God of Jacob – 20:1
Oh My Strength – 22:19
King of Glory – 29:3
Oh Lord God of Truth 31:5
The Lord God of Israel – 41:13
Oh Mighty One -45:3
The King of all the earth – 47:7
God of Abraham – 47:9
God of the Most High – 57:2
YAH -68:4
The Almighty – 68:14
God the Lord – 68:20
Oh Holy One of Israel – 71:22
Oh Shepherd of Israel – 80:1
The Lord our Maker – 95:6
God their Savior – 106:21
The Mighty One of Jacob – 132:2
The God of Gods – 136:2
The God of heaven – 136:26

Descriptions of God in the Book of Psalms
A shield for me – 3:3
My glory – 3:3
The One who lifts up my head – 3:3
The righteous God – 7:9
A just judge – 7:11
A refuge – 9:9
The portion of my inheritance and my cup – 16:5
My strength – 18:1
The Lord is my rock and my fortress and my deliverer – 18:2
The horn of my salvation, stronghold – 18:2
My support – 18:18
My shepherd – 23:1
My light and my salvation – 27:1
The strength of my life – 27:1
The saving refuge of His anointed – 28:8
My helper – 30:10
Rock of refuge – 31:2
My hiding place – 32:7
My help and my deliverer – 41:17
The God of my life – 42:8
My exceeding joy – 43:4
A very present help in trouble 46:1
Our guide even to death – 48:14
My defense – 59:9
My God of mercy – 59:10
A shelter of me, a strong tower from the enemy – 61:3
A father of the fatherless, a defender of widows – 68:5
The strength of my heart and my portion forever – 73:26

The great God and the great King above all gods – 95:3

He who keeps Israel – 121:4

Your shade at your right hand – 121:5

My portion in the land of the living – 142:5

My high tower – 144:2

Work those titles and descriptions of God into your fervent prayers and into your worship and watch what God does to the powers of darkness when they try to assail you.

One more thing: just read that list out loud and watch what it does to your spirit. Can you say, "boom"?

PSALM 59 (KJV)

1 Deliver me from mine enemies, O my God: defend me from them that rise up against me.

2 Deliver me from the workers of iniquity, and save me from bloody men.

3 For, lo, they lie in wait for my soul: the mighty are gathered against me; not for my transgression, nor for my sin, O Lord.

4 They run and prepare themselves without my fault: awake to help me, and behold.

5 Thou therefore, O Lord God of hosts, the God of Israel, awake to visit all the heathen: be not merciful to any wicked transgressors. Selah.

6 They return at evening: they make a noise like a dog, and go round about the city.

7 Behold, they belch out with their mouth: swords are in their lips: for who, say they, doth hear?

Psalms of War

8 But thou, O Lord, shalt laugh at them; thou shalt have all the heathen in derision.

9 Because of his strength will I wait upon thee: for God is my defence.

10 The God of my mercy shall prevent me: God shall let me see my desire upon mine enemies.

11 Slay them not, lest my people forget: scatter them by thy power; and bring them down, O Lord our shield.

12 For the sin of their mouth and the words of their lips let them even be taken in their pride: and for cursing and lying which they speak.

13 Consume them in wrath, consume them, that they may not be: and let them know that God ruleth in Jacob unto the ends of the earth. Selah.

14 And at evening let them return; and let them make a noise like a dog, and go round about the city.

15 Let them wander up and down for meat, and grudge if they be not satisfied.

16 But I will sing of thy power; yea, I will sing aloud of thy mercy in the morning: for thou hast been my defence and refuge in the day of my trouble.

17 Unto thee, O my strength, will I sing: for God is my defence, and the God of my mercy.

Chapter Eighteen: A Psalm of War Against those Who Try to Ruin Your Name

The King James Version of the Bible, in Psalm 63:11, states … "But the king shall rejoice in God; every one that sweareth by him shall glory: but the mouth of them that speak lies shall be stopped."

Eugene Peterson translates that passage this way in The Message Bible … "But the king is glad in God; his true friends spread the joy, while small-minded gossips are gagged for good." (TM)

Small-minded gossips are gagged for good?

Hahahahahahahahahahaha!

I. LOVE. THAT.

Gossip is something you don't hear condemned much in the church anymore, because little "Christian" punks are filled with this demon. Thus, they won't preach against it, or confess it, because that would expose what a pusillanimous tattletale they've become.

Pastors are the worst gossipers on the planet.

David called the gossiper a "small-minded person."

A small-minded dork is someone who's narrow-minded, petty, intolerant, and mean.

Here's an FYI: Everywhere gossip is mentioned in the scripture it's always grouped up with some of the grossest vices known to mankind (See Romans 1:29, 2Corinthians 12:20; 1Timothy 3:11, 1Timothy 5:13, 2Timothy 3:3 and Titus 2:3. Check out those scriptures. I dare you. (Here's how you know if you have a gossip demon living inside of you: you won't look up those scriptures and you sure as heck won't memorize them or put them on your refrigerator.)

David's boy, Solomon, says in Proverbs 20:19 that the believer should not associate with a gossip. Translation: ditch the pea-brains who talk smack about other people.

David said that gossip is the trait of the damned (Psalm 63:9).

God help us.

PSALM 63 (KJV)

1 O God, thou art my God; early will I seek thee: my soul thirsteth for thee, my flesh longeth for thee in a dry and thirsty land, where no water is;

2 To see thy power and thy glory, so as I have seen thee in the sanctuary.

Psalms of War

3 Because thy lovingkindness is better than life, my lips shall praise thee.

4 Thus will I bless thee while I live: I will lift up my hands in thy name.

5 My soul shall be satisfied as with marrow and fatness; and my mouth shall praise thee with joyful lips:

6 When I remember thee upon my bed, and meditate on thee in the night watches.

7 Because thou hast been my help, therefore in the shadow of thy wings will I rejoice.

8 My soul followeth hard after thee: thy right hand upholdeth me.

9 But those that seek my soul, to destroy it, shall go into the lower parts of the earth.

10 They shall fall by the sword: they shall be a portion for foxes.

11 But the king shall rejoice in God; every one that sweareth by him shall glory: but the mouth of them that speak lies shall be stopped.

Chapter Nineteen: A Psalm of War Against All Enemies of God

If you listen to a lot of believers nowadays, they're always talking about the power of the Devil, the power of evil, and the pervasiveness of perversion.

In other words, there's a big Anti-Christ and a small Jesus Christ.

Now, granted, they won't say those exact words but that's how they speak. Like there's not a Badass God that we serve who can kick some major, and I mean, major demonic and evil peoples' backsides.

David didn't have a pipsqueak view of God and that was way before the resurrection and ascension when ALL authority in heaven and earth was given to Jesus Christ and not the Devil. Hello.

Indeed, in Psalm 68, David said that God …

1. Scattered enemies.
2. Melts 'em like wax.
3. Makes 'em perish in His presence.
4. Shakes the earth.
5. Makes kings of armies flee.
6. Scatters kings.
7. Has thousands upon thousands of warring angels.
8. Takes captive captivity.
9. Daily loads us down with benefits.
10. Wounds the head of the enemy.
11. Is "terrible" in His strength and power.

Is that how you hear little Christians describe God today? No? I didn't think so. But that's how David described his awesome God. Y'know ... the God of the Bible? Enjoy and share Psalm 68 with people who need a bigger image of God.

Psalm 68 (KJV)

1 Let God arise, let his enemies be scattered: let them also that hate him flee before him.

2 As smoke is driven away, so drive them away: as wax melteth before the fire, so let the wicked perish at the presence of God.

3 But let the righteous be glad; let them rejoice before God: yea, let them exceedingly rejoice.

4 Sing unto God, sing praises to his name: extol him that rideth upon the heavens by his name Jah, and rejoice before him.

5 A father of the fatherless, and a judge of the widows,

Psalms of War

is God in his holy habitation.

6 God setteth the solitary in families: he bringeth out those which are bound with chains: but the rebellious dwell in a dry land.

7 O God, when thou wentest forth before thy people, when thou didst march through the wilderness; Selah:

8 The earth shook, the heavens also dropped at the presence of God: even Sinai itself was moved at the presence of God, the God of Israel.

9 Thou, O God, didst send a plentiful rain, whereby thou didst confirm thine inheritance, when it was weary.

10 Thy congregation hath dwelt therein: thou, O God, hast prepared of thy goodness for the poor.

11 The Lord gave the word: great was the company of those that published it.

12 Kings of armies did flee apace: and she that tarried at home divided the spoil.

13 Though ye have lien among the pots, yet shall ye be as the wings of a dove covered with silver, and her feathers with yellow gold.

14 When the Almighty scattered kings in it, it was white as snow in Salmon.

15 The hill of God is as the hill of Bashan; an high hill as the hill of Bashan.

16 Why leap ye, ye high hills? this is the hill which God desireth to dwell in; yea, the Lord will dwell in it for ever.

17 The chariots of God are twenty thousand, even thousands of angels: the Lord is among them, as in Sinai, in

the holy place.

18 Thou hast ascended on high, thou hast led captivity captive: thou hast received gifts for men; yea, for the rebellious also, that the Lord God might dwell among them.

19 Blessed be the Lord, who daily loadeth us with benefits, even the God of our salvation. Selah.

20 He that is our God is the God of salvation; and unto God the Lord belong the issues from death.

21 But God shall wound the head of his enemies, and the hairy scalp of such an one as goeth on still in his trespasses.

22 The Lord said, I will bring again from Bashan, I will bring my people again from the depths of the sea:

23 That thy foot may be dipped in the blood of thine enemies, and the tongue of thy dogs in the same.

24 They have seen thy goings, O God; even the goings of my God, my King, in the sanctuary.

25 The singers went before, the players on instruments followed after; among them were the damsels playing with timbrels.

26 Bless ye God in the congregations, even the Lord, from the fountain of Israel.

27 There is little Benjamin with their ruler, the princes of Judah and their council, the princes of Zebulun, and the princes of Naphtali.

28 Thy God hath commanded thy strength: strengthen, O God, that which thou hast wrought for us.

29 Because of thy temple at Jerusalem shall kings bring presents unto thee.

Psalms of War

30 Rebuke the company of spearmen, the multitude of the bulls, with the calves of the people, till every one submit himself with pieces of silver: scatter thou the people that delight in war.

31 Princes shall come out of Egypt; Ethiopia shall soon stretch out her hands unto God.

32 Sing unto God, ye kingdoms of the earth; O sing praises unto the Lord; Selah:

33 To him that rideth upon the heavens of heavens, which were of old; lo, he doth send out his voice, and that a mighty voice.

34 Ascribe ye strength unto God: his excellency is over Israel, and his strength is in the clouds.

35 O God, thou art terrible out of thy holy places: the God of Israel is he that giveth strength and power unto his people. Blessed be God.

Chapter Twenty: A Psalm of War Against those Who Hate You Without Cause

Have you ever had people, that you have never met, hate you for no personal reason?
It's weird, eh?

That's the world we live in today in the United States of Liberal Acrimony. Hate is the soup du jour all day, every day.

David had that problem many moons ago. He said, "They that hate me without a cause are more than the hairs of mine head: they that would destroy me, being mine enemies wrongfully, are mighty. (Psalm 69:4)

Jesus said, if you follow Me, you're going to be hated (John 15:18).

You know what people don't like in today's "please like my Facebook/IG post" world of fetid feebleness? The thought of not being liked, that's what.

People hated David for being successful.

They hated David for being sinful.

His brothers hated him because he exposed their fear and weakness before Goliath.

He was an alien to his brothers.

Most people would cry and blather on for the next fifty years about not being loved, but David didn't. David said he let zeal for God's house consume him (Psalm 69:9) not whether he was liked or not by his myopic brothers or the contemporary jackasses that surrounded him.

What David prays on the impenitents' heads here in Psalm 69 is pretty wild.

Do you know what I am about to type next?

Here it is ...

I bet you never heard Psalm 69 sung, prayed, or preached on in your youth group.

PSALM 69 (KJV)

1 Save me, O God, For the waters have threatened my life.

2 I have sunk in deep mire, and there is no foothold; I have come into deep waters, and a flood overflows me.

3 I am weary with my crying; my throat is parched; My eyes fail while I wait for my God.

4 Those who hate me without a cause are more than the hairs of my head; Those who would destroy me are

Psalms of War

powerful, being wrongfully my enemies; What I did not steal, I then have to restore.

5 O God, it is You who knows my folly, And my wrongs are not hidden from You.

6 May those who wait for You not be ashamed through me, O Lord God of hosts; May those who seek You not be dishonored through me, O God of Israel,

7 Because for Your sake I have borne reproach; Dishonor has covered my face.

8 I have become estranged from my brothers And an alien to my mother's sons.

9 For zeal for Your house has consumed me, And the reproaches of those who reproach You have fallen on me.

10 When I wept in my soul with fasting, It became my reproach.

11 When I made sackcloth my clothing, I became a byword to them.

12 Those who sit in the gate talk about me, And I *am* the song of the drunkards.

13 But as for me, my prayer is to You, O Lord, at an acceptable time; O God, in the greatness of Your lovingkindness, Answer me with Your saving truth.

14 Deliver me from the mire and do not let me sink; May I be delivered from my foes and from the deep waters.

15 May the flood of water not overflow me Nor the deep swallow me up, Nor the pit shut its mouth on me.

16 Answer me, O Lord, for Your lovingkindness is good; According to the greatness of Your compassion,

turn to me,

17 And do not hide Your face from Your servant, For I am in distress; answer me quickly.

18 Oh draw near to my soul *and* redeem it; Ransom me because of my enemies!

19 You know my reproach and my shame and my dishonor; All my adversaries are before You.

20 Reproach has broken my heart and I am so sick. And I looked for sympathy, but there was none, And for comforters, but I found none.

21 They also gave me gall for my food And for my thirst they gave me vinegar to drink.

22 May their table before them become a snare; And when they are in peace, *may it become* a trap.

23 May their eyes grow dim so that they cannot see, And make their loins shake continually.

24 Pour out Your indignation on them, And may Your burning anger overtake them.

25 May their camp be desolate; May none dwell in their tents.

26 For they have persecuted him whom You Yourself have smitten, And they tell of the pain of those whom You have wounded.

27 Add iniquity to their iniquity, And may they not come into Your righteousness.

28 May they be blotted out of the book of life And may they not be recorded with the righteous.

29 But I am afflicted and in pain; May Your salvation, O God, set me *securely* on high.

Psalms of War

30 I will praise the name of God with song And magnify Him with thanksgiving. **31** And it will please the Lord better than an ox *Or* a young bull with horns and hoofs.

32 The humble have seen *it and* are glad; You who seek God, let your heart revive.

33 For the Lord hears the needy And does not despise His *who are* prisoners.

34 Let heaven and earth praise Him, The seas and everything that moves in them.

35 For God will save Zion and build the cities of Judah, That they may dwell there and possess it.

36 The descendants of His servants will inherit it, And those who love His name will dwell in it.

Chapter Twenty One: A Psalm of War Against those Who Want God to Forsake You

You know who, or what, rather, I never want to become? I don't want to become someone who longs for someone else's demise.

Sure, I have enemies.

If you stand for something -- anything, nowadays -- you will have enemies.

That said, I don't daydream about them going broke, or becoming unsuccessful, or getting some horrible disease and dying.

I don't want to be that dude.

Now, for clarification: I don't wish the Devil, heretics, anti-theistic jackanapes, or soulless politicians well. I hope God crushes their satanic devices, in time and on this *terra firma*. That said, those who're ignorantly caught up in Satan's BS I truly hope they get freed from his ubiquitous snares.

Who the heck wants to be the sick little weasel who seeks after someone's demise? Who hopes that God would wreck their soul ... that longs for life to wipe them out?

David had these types of ill-wishing critters in abundance who greatly served el Diablo's desire for David's ruin. David asked God to shame and confuse these idiots in Psalm 70 and so should you.

P<small>SALM</small> 70 (KJV)

1 Make haste, o God, to deliver me; make haste to help me, O Lord.

2 Let them be ashamed and confounded that seek after my soul: let them be turned backward, and put to confusion, that desire my hurt.

3 Let them be turned back for a reward of their shame that say, Aha, aha.

4 Let all those that seek thee rejoice and be glad in thee: and let such as love thy salvation say continually, Let God be magnified.

5 But I am poor and needy: make haste unto me, O God: thou art my help and my deliverer; O Lord, make no tarrying.

Psalms of War

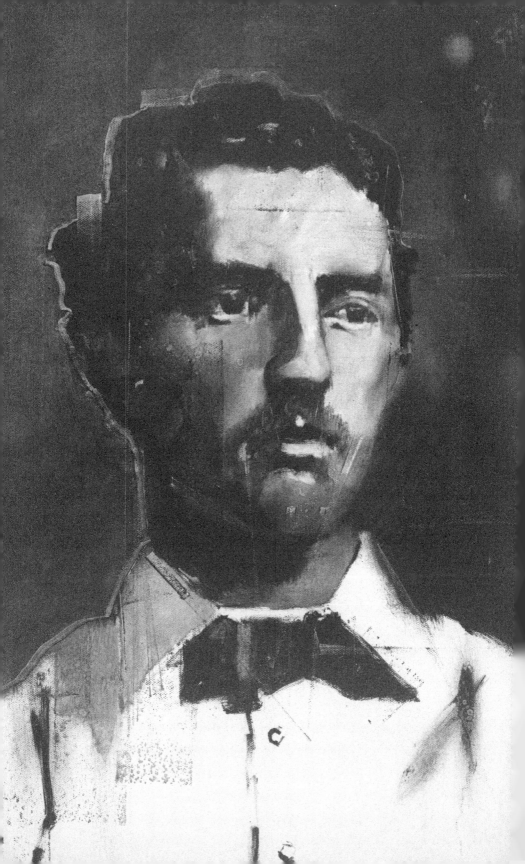

Chapter Twenty Two: A Psalm of War Against Forces Fighting Against the Church

My wife and I have been very blessed to personally know some epic men of God. Some of them are still alive and kicking.

What all of them had in common as octogenarians, was that they were still on fire for God in their latter days.

Their mind was sharp.

Their strength was not abated.

They preach(ed) with clarity, unction, and zeal.

They were not in retirement mode.

I don't even understand how one can "retire" from preaching.

Anyway ...

These gents maintained a Holy Ghost volatility way up into the grey-headed days.

In Psalm 71 the psalmist asks God, "... when I am old and greyheaded, O God, forsake me not; until I have shewed thy strength unto this generation, and thy power to every one that is to come."

The psalmist wants God to give him strength to pass the baton of God's power to the next generation.

Please note: he wasn't focused on vacations. He wasn't monitoring his blood pressure. He wasn't sitting on a bedpan in an old folks' home. He was vibrant and active in Kingdom concerns.

As you read Psalm 71 ask yourself, when was the last time you heard an old Christian man or woman remotely sound like this?

PSALM 71 (KJV)

1 In thee, O Lord, do I put my trust: let me never be put to confusion.

2 Deliver me in thy righteousness, and cause me to escape: incline thine ear unto me, and save me.

3 Be thou my strong habitation, whereunto I may continually resort: thou hast given commandment to save me; for thou art my rock and my fortress.

4 Deliver me, O my God, out of the hand of the wicked, out of the hand of the unrighteous and cruel man.

5 For thou art my hope, O Lord God: thou art my trust

Psalms of War

from my youth.

6 By thee have I been holden up from the womb: thou art he that took me out of my mother's bowels: my praise shall be continually of thee.

7 I am as a wonder unto many; but thou art my strong refuge.

8 Let my mouth be filled with thy praise and with thy honour all the day.

9 Cast me not off in the time of old age; forsake me not when my strength faileth.

10 For mine enemies speak against me; and they that lay wait for my soul take counsel together,

11 Saying, God hath forsaken him: persecute and take him; for there is none to deliver him.

12 O God, be not far from me: O my God, make haste for my help.

13 Let them be confounded and consumed that are adversaries to my soul; let them be covered with reproach and dishonour that seek my hurt.

14 But I will hope continually, and will yet praise thee more and more.

15 My mouth shall shew forth thy righteousness and thy salvation all the day; for I know not the numbers thereof.

16 I will go in the strength of the Lord God: I will make mention of thy righteousness, even of thine only.

17 O God, thou hast taught me from my youth: and hitherto have I declared thy wondrous works.

18 Now also when I am old and greyheaded, O God, forsake me not; until I have shewed thy strength unto

this generation, and thy power to every one that is to come.

19 Thy righteousness also, O God, is very high, who hast done great things: O God, who is like unto thee!

20 Thou, which hast shewed me great and sore troubles, shalt quicken me again, and shalt bring me up again from the depths of the earth.

21 Thou shalt increase my greatness, and comfort me on every side.

22 I will also praise thee with the psaltery, even thy truth, O my God: unto thee will I sing with the harp, O thou Holy One of Israel.

23 My lips shall greatly rejoice when I sing unto thee; and my soul, which thou hast redeemed.

24 My tongue also shall talk of thy righteousness all the day long: for they are confounded, for they are brought unto shame, that seek my hurt.

Psalms of War

Chapter Twenty Three: A Psalm of War Against Enemies Infiltrating the Body of Christ

In our current ecclesiastical milieu, demons can waltz right in, set up shop and operate, unhindered, in most evangelical and catholic churches.

Yep, demons and the dolts controlled by them, can spew their bullcrap, parade their damnable "lifestyle" and ignore the scripture with impunity and it's okey dokey with a lot of churches and pastors.

Not so, under King David. Oh, heck no.

In Psalm 74, when the enemy started wreaking havoc inside the sanctuary of God, David's chief musician, Asaph, went on the offense and rained down hellfire with this epic imprecatory Psalm.

If you see Satan weaving his way into your local church or denomination, then dust this Psalm off and launch it up the enemy's tailpipe.

PSALM 74 (KJV)

1 O God, why hast thou cast us off for ever? why doth thine anger smoke against the sheep of thy pasture?

2 Remember thy congregation, which thou hast purchased of old; the rod of thine inheritance, which thou hast redeemed; this mount Zion, wherein thou hast dwelt.

3 Lift up thy feet unto the perpetual desolations; even all that the enemy hath done wickedly in the sanctuary.

4 Thine enemies roar in the midst of thy congregations; they set up their ensigns for signs.

5 A man was famous according as he had lifted up axes upon the thick trees.

6 But now they break down the carved work thereof at once with axes and hammers.

7 They have cast fire into thy sanctuary, they have defiled by casting down the dwelling place of thy name to the ground.

8 They said in their hearts, Let us destroy them together: they have burned up all the synagogues of God in the land.

9 We see not our signs: there is no more any prophet: neither is there among us any that knoweth how long.

Psalms of War

10 O God, how long shall the adversary reproach? shall the enemy blaspheme thy name for ever?

11 Why withdrawest thou thy hand, even thy right hand? pluck it out of thy bosom.

12 For God is my King of old, working salvation in the midst of the earth.

13 Thou didst divide the sea by thy strength: thou brakest the heads of the dragons in the waters.

14 Thou brakest the heads of leviathan in pieces, and gavest him to be meat to the people inhabiting the wilderness.

15 Thou didst cleave the fountain and the flood: thou driedst up mighty rivers.

16 The day is thine, the night also is thine: thou hast prepared the light and the sun.

17 Thou hast set all the borders of the earth: thou hast made summer and winter.

18 Remember this, that the enemy hath reproached, O Lord, and that the foolish people have blasphemed thy name.

19 O deliver not the soul of thy turtledove unto the multitude of the wicked: forget not the congregation of thy poor for ever.

20 Have respect unto the covenant: for the dark places of the earth are full of the habitations of cruelty.

21 O let not the oppressed return ashamed: let the poor and needy praise thy name.

22 Arise, O God, plead thine own cause: remember how the foolish man reproacheth thee daily.

23 Forget not the voice of thine enemies: the tumult of

those that rise up against thee increaseth continually.

Psalms of War

Chapter Twenty Four: A Psalm of War Against those Who Exalt Themselves Above God

The wrath of God.

There's a subject that gets about as much attention in Church today as Rosie O'Donnell's treadmill does at her house.

Lots of pastors won't touch this topic with a ten-foot pew because it is "too negative" and not very "seeker sensitive".

In other words, they're wussies, driven by the approval of men, and governed not by the Holy Spirit, but demon spirits, sent to deceive people who like their ears tickled and thus plunging them into an everlasting hell.

The Bible, on the other hand, talks a lot about the wrath of God. And that includes the New Testament where heretical pastors tell us God has changed and isn't this mean old God anymore but has morphed into a sweet socialist who wears sandals and has a universal view on salvation.

My foul flesh would love the aforementioned to be true, but alas, it's bunkum.

Indeed, the wrath of God flowed through the hermeneutical filter of the Cross right into the Gospels and the rest of the New Testament.

The letter to The Romans mentions the wrath of God nine times and the book of Revelation mentions the wrath of God thirteen times.

In Psalm 79, Asaph, asks God to pay back the enemies of God "sevenfold" (or seven times) the reproach, wherewith they have reproached God."

Yes, dear Christian, God does execute His holy and just wrath against the impenitent and implacable who have cursed Christ and spurned His people.

And Psalm 79 is the 24th example of that which has been spotlighted in this book.

Oh, one more thing.

While you're memorizing John 3:16, also commit to memory John 3:36, "He that believeth on the Son hath everlasting life: and he that believeth not the Son shall not see life; but the wrath of God abideth on him."

By the way, Jesus said both John 3:16 and John 3:36.

Psalms of War

PSALM 79 (KJV)

1 O god, the heathen are come into thine inheritance; thy holy temple have they defiled; they have laid Jerusalem on heaps.

2 The dead bodies of thy servants have they given to be meat unto the fowls of the heaven, the flesh of thy saints unto the beasts of the earth.

3 Their blood have they shed like water round about Jerusalem; and there was none to bury them.

4 We are become a reproach to our neighbours, a scorn and derision to them that are round about us.

5 How long, Lord? wilt thou be angry for ever? shall thy jealousy burn like fire?

6 Pour out thy wrath upon the heathen that have not known thee, and upon the kingdoms that have not called upon thy name.

7 For they have devoured Jacob, and laid waste his dwelling place.

8 O remember not against us former iniquities: let thy tender mercies speedily prevent us: for we are brought very low.

9 Help us, O God of our salvation, for the glory of thy name: and deliver us, and purge away our sins, for thy name's sake.

10 Wherefore should the heathen say, Where is their God? let him be known among the heathen in our sight by the revenging of the blood of thy servants which is shed.

11 Let the sighing of the prisoner come before thee; according to the greatness of thy power preserve thou

those that are appointed to die;

12 And render unto our neighbours sevenfold into their bosom their reproach, wherewith they have reproached thee, O Lord.

13 So we thy people and sheep of thy pasture will give thee thanks for ever: we will shew forth thy praise to all generations.

Psalms of War

Chapter Twenty Five: A Psalm of War Against Anti-Christian Blowhards

China hates America. Iran's no fan either.

Ditto with Russia.

And mega-dittos regarding George Soros.

Yes, America and her Constitution, Bill of Rights, and our Declaration of Independence are a thing of fear and loathing for our enemies foreign and domestic.

The true Church also draws deep disdain from the aforementioned, and you can add to that list Marxist radicals who've embraced an anti-theistic worldview of stupidity on steroids.

Indeed, these ideological bedfellows don't like those who call upon the Lord with an unfeigned faith and from a pure heart.

Ergo, they plot to do the Church in. They conspire how to crush us. They'd like to see us wiped off the face of this earth with the Church's name scratched off the books.

That's where Psalm 83 comes in real handy.

Asaph, in Psalm 83, prays to God to do this to their new set of enemies what God did to the old set of enemies such as, Edom, Moab, Gebal, Ammon, Amalek, Philistia, the Tyrians, Assyria, and the Midianites.

Google what God did to His people's enemies who wouldn't leave His Chosen Ones alone. It wasn't pretty.

Psalm 83:13-18 is what the Church should pray against the powers of darkness and their earthly ilk who persecute the church and will not repent.

PSALM 83 (KJV)

1 Keep not thou silence, O God: hold not thy peace, and be not still, O God.

2 For, lo, thine enemies make a tumult: and they that hate thee have lifted up the head.

3 They have taken crafty counsel against thy people, and consulted against thy hidden ones.

4 They have said, Come, and let us cut them off from being a nation; that the name of Israel may be no more in remembrance.

5 For they have consulted together with one consent: they are confederate against thee:

6 The tabernacles of Edom, and the Ishmaelites; of

Psalms of War

Moab, and the Hagarenes;

7 Gebal, and Ammon, and Amalek; the Philistines with the inhabitants of Tyre;

8 Assur also is joined with them: they have holpen the children of Lot. Selah.

9 Do unto them as unto the Midianites; as to Sisera, as to Jabin, at the brook of Kison:

10 Which perished at Endor: they became as dung for the earth.

11 Make their nobles like Oreb, and like Zeeb: yea, all their princes as Zebah, and as Zalmunna:

12 Who said, Let us take to ourselves the houses of God in possession.

13 O my God, make them like a wheel; as the stubble before the wind.

14 As the fire burneth a wood, and as the flame setteth the mountains on fire;

15 So persecute them with thy tempest, and make them afraid with thy storm.

16 Fill their faces with shame; that they may seek thy name, O Lord.

17 Let them be confounded and troubled for ever; yea, let them be put to shame, and perish:

18 That men may know that thou, whose name alone is Jehovah, art the most high over all the earth.

Chapter Twenty Six: A Psalm of War Against those Who Make Life a Living Hell

Dear Demons and Those of You Controlled by Them: Do you think that the God who created the ear doesn't hear your threats leveled against His people?

In addition, do you believe the God who created your beady eyes doesn't see what you're doing to His people?

If you do think He can see and hear what you're doing and planning to do against the people of God, then you are this thing called, "nuttier than a squirrel turd."

Doug Giles

Please allow Psalm 94 to wake you up to your impending doom if you don't cease and desist your harassment of the saints. Enjoy.

PSALM 94 (KJV)

1 O Lord God, to whom vengeance belongeth; O God, to whom vengeance belongeth, shew thyself.

2 Lift up thyself, thou judge of the earth: render a reward to the proud.

3 Lord, how long shall the wicked, how long shall the wicked triumph?

4 How long shall they utter and speak hard things? and all the workers of iniquity boast themselves?

5 They break in pieces thy people, O Lord, and afflict thine heritage.

6 They slay the widow and the stranger, and murder the fatherless.

7 Yet they say, The Lord shall not see, neither shall the God of Jacob regard it.

8 Understand, ye brutish among the people: and ye fools, when will ye be wise?

9 He that planted the ear, shall he not hear? he that formed the eye, shall he not see?

10 He that chastiseth the heathen, shall not he correct? he that teacheth man knowledge, shall not he know?

11 The Lord knoweth the thoughts of man, that they are vanity.

12 Blessed is the man whom thou chastenest, O Lord, and teachest him out of thy law;

Psalms of War

13 That thou mayest give him rest from the days of adversity, until the pit be digged for the wicked.

14 For the Lord will not cast off his people, neither will he forsake his inheritance.

15 But judgment shall return unto righteousness: and all the upright in heart shall follow it.

16 Who will rise up for me against the evildoers? or who will stand up for me against the workers of iniquity?

17 Unless the Lord had been my help, my soul had almost dwelt in silence.

18 When I said, My foot slippeth; thy mercy, O Lord, held me up.

19 In the multitude of my thoughts within me thy comforts delight my soul.

20 Shall the throne of iniquity have fellowship with thee, which frameth mischief by a law?

21 They gather themselves together against the soul of the righteous, and condemn the innocent blood.

22 But the Lord is my defence; and my God is the rock of my refuge.

23 And he shall bring upon them their own iniquity, and shall cut them off in their own wickedness; yea, the Lord our God shall cut them off.

Chapter Twenty Seven : A Psalm of War Against those Who Make Everything Suck

I know this book has been heavy.

The themes of wrath, warfare, demons, battles, satanic schemes, attacks from men and devils can be brutal on the genteel psyche of the dainty Christian who was not told upon confession and baptism that they were born again into a raging spiritual war that's been cookin' since the creation of man.

Welcome to the jungle, Dinky. May I take your coat?

That said, God knows we can handle only so much, and even as we do war in the heavenlies, He provides for us greatly and sustains us utterly while we're kicking butt and taking names on His behalf while we're here on this blue marble.

In Psalm 94, the psalmist describes the power and the majesty of The One who goes before us and The One who has our six. Read it. It's awesome.

What I get from this glorious song is, no matter what I face, even the Devil himself, my God is infinitely more powerful and thus, I'm going to be more than okay in life and death.

Or as Paul put it, "Who shall separate us from the love of Christ? shall tribulation, or distress, or persecution, or famine, or nakedness, or peril, or sword? As it is written, For thy sake we are killed all the day long; we are accounted as sheep for the slaughter. Nay, in all these things we are more than conquerors through him that loved us. For I am persuaded, that neither death, nor life, nor angels, nor principalities, nor powers, nor things present, nor things to come, nor height, nor depth, nor any other creature, shall be able to separate us from the love of God, which is in Christ Jesus our Lord." - Romans 8:35-39 (KJV)

PSALM 104 (KJV)

1 Bless the Lord, O my soul. O Lord my God, thou art very great; thou art clothed with honour and majesty.

2 Who coverest thyself with light as with a garment: who stretchest out the heavens like a curtain:

3 Who layeth the beams of his chambers in the waters: who maketh the clouds his chariot: who walketh upon the wings of the wind:

4 Who maketh his angels spirits; his ministers a flaming fire:

5 Who laid the foundations of the earth, that it should not be removed for ever.

6 Thou coveredst it with the deep as with a garment:

Psalms of War

the waters stood above the mountains.

7 At thy rebuke they fled; at the voice of thy thunder they hasted away.

8 They go up by the mountains; they go down by the valleys unto the place which thou hast founded for them.

9 Thou hast set a bound that they may not pass over; that they turn not again to cover the earth.

10 He sendeth the springs into the valleys, which run among the hills.

11 They give drink to every beast of the field: the wild asses quench their thirst.

12 By them shall the fowls of the heaven have their habitation, which sing among the branches.

13 He watereth the hills from his chambers: the earth is satisfied with the fruit of thy works.

14 He causeth the grass to grow for the cattle, and herb for the service of man: that he may bring forth food out of the earth;

15 And wine that maketh glad the heart of man, and oil to make his face to shine, and bread which strengtheneth man's heart.

16 The trees of the Lord are full of sap; the cedars of Lebanon, which he hath planted;

17 Where the birds make their nests: as for the stork, the fir trees are her house.

18 The high hills are a refuge for the wild goats; and the rocks for the conies.

19 He appointed the moon for seasons: the sun knoweth his going down.

20 Thou makest darkness, and it is night: wherein all the beasts of the forest do creep forth.

21 The young lions roar after their prey, and seek their meat from God.

22 The sun ariseth, they gather themselves together, and lay them down in their dens.

23 Man goeth forth unto his work and to his labour until the evening.

24 O Lord, how manifold are thy works! in wisdom hast thou made them all: the earth is full of thy riches.

25 So is this great and wide sea, wherein are things creeping innumerable, both small and great beasts.

26 There go the ships: there is that leviathan, whom thou hast made to play therein.

27 These wait all upon thee; that thou mayest give them their meat in due season.

28 That thou givest them they gather: thou openest thine hand, they are filled with good.

29 Thou hidest thy face, they are troubled: thou takest away their breath, they die, and return to their dust.

30 Thou sendest forth thy spirit, they are created: and thou renewest the face of the earth.

31 The glory of the Lord shall endure for ever: the Lord shall rejoice in his works.

32 He looketh on the earth, and it trembleth: he toucheth the hills, and they smoke.

33 I will sing unto the Lord as long as I live: I will sing praise to my God while I have my being.

34 My meditation of him shall be sweet: I will be glad

Psalms of War

in the Lord.

35 Let the sinners be consumed out of the earth, and let the wicked be no more. Bless thou the Lord, O my soul. Praise ye the Lord.

Chapter Twenty Eight: A Psalm of War Against those Who Lie About You

This has got to be one of the most brutal prayers/songs in the entire *verbum Dei* and yet, it was inspired by the Holy Spirit and is profitable for New Testament peeps, at least according to the equally inspired Apostle Paul (2Timothy 3:16; Romans 15:4).

Theologians call this song the "Judas Psalm" because what happened here in Psalm 109 is what happened to that ratfink, Judas Iscariot.

"Let his days be few; and let another take his office" (Psalm 109:8) was quoted by the Apostle Peter before the apostles elected the replacement for Judas Iscariot in Acts 1:16–20 after he committed suicide.

Verses twelve and thirteen in Psalm 109 contain some of the most brutal imprecations in the Bible. No joke. Read 'em for yourself.

This psalm is dealing with an obvious deceitful impenitent jackass, and I use jackass in the biblical sense of the word (Job 11:12; Psalm 32:9). We're talking about a liar, a scalawag, a prevaricating foe who's trying to do in a faithful follower of God.

The psalmist, under duress, asks God to sort this liar out and do it in the most terrifying manner.

To me, the hinge pin of this psalm seems to be the obstreperous' devotion to cursing someone who loved them (Psalm 109:4).

Now, when the Bible says someone is cursing, it is not talking about someone dropping the F-Bomb when they hit their thumb trying to hammer a nail or if someone called a dude's mom a pirate hooker, because she's been married more times than Liz Taylor, but rather the wishing of ill upon another person or spreading falsehoods about them. Y'know … they're satanic gossips.

Anyway …

According to Psalm 109:17, the psalmist said he LOVED cursing. He loved wishing ill. He loved spreading falsehoods so cursing came to him. Since he delighted not in blessing people, the blessings were removed far from him.

Here's an idea. Next time you're at youth group, ask the youth pastor to read this psalm aloud and have the kiddos discuss it? Or maybe have the women's bible study or the manly man's group at church give it a gander one month?

Here's Psalm 109.

Psalms of War

PSALM 109 (KJV)

1 Hold not thy peace, O God of my praise;

2 For the mouth of the wicked and the mouth of the deceitful are opened against me: they have spoken against me with a lying tongue.

3 They compassed me about also with words of hatred; and fought against me without a cause.

4 For my love they are my adversaries: but I give myself unto prayer.

5 And they have rewarded me evil for good, and hatred for my love.

6 Set thou a wicked man over him: and let Satan stand at his right hand.

7 When he shall be judged, let him be condemned: and let his prayer become sin.

8 Let his days be few; and let another take his office.

9 Let his children be fatherless, and his wife a widow.

10 Let his children be continually vagabonds, and beg: let them seek their bread also out of their desolate places.

11 Let the extortioner catch all that he hath; and let the strangers spoil his labour.

12 Let there be none to extend mercy unto him: neither let there be any to favour his fatherless children.

13 Let his posterity be cut off; and in the generation following let their name be blotted out.

14 Let the iniquity of his fathers be remembered with the Lord; and let not the sin of his mother be blotted out.

15 Let them be before the Lord continually, that he may cut off the memory of them from the earth.

16 Because that he remembered not to shew mercy, but persecuted the poor and needy man, that he might even slay the broken in heart.

17 As he loved cursing, so let it come unto him: as he delighted not in blessing, so let it be far from him.

18 As he clothed himself with cursing like as with his garment, so let it come into his bowels like water, and like oil into his bones.

19 Let it be unto him as the garment which covereth him, and for a girdle wherewith he is girded continually.

20 Let this be the reward of mine adversaries from the Lord, and of them that speak evil against my soul.

21 But do thou for me, O God the Lord, for thy name's sake: because thy mercy is good, deliver thou me.

22 For I am poor and needy, and my heart is wounded within me.

23 I am gone like the shadow when it declineth: I am tossed up and down as the locust.

24 My knees are weak through fasting; and my flesh faileth of fatness.

25 I became also a reproach unto them: when they looked upon me they shaked their heads.

26 Help me, O Lord my God: O save me according to thy mercy:

Psalms of War

27 That they may know that this is thy hand; that thou, Lord, hast done it.

28 Let them curse, but bless thou: when they arise, let them be ashamed; but let thy servant rejoice.

29 Let mine adversaries be clothed with shame, and let them cover themselves with their own confusion, as with a mantle.

30 I will greatly praise the Lord with my mouth; yea, I will praise him among the multitude.

31 For he shall stand at the right hand of the poor, to save him from those that condemn his soul.

Doug Giles

About the Author

Doug earned his Bachelor of Fine Arts degree from Texas Tech University and his certificates in both Theological and Biblical Studies from Knox Theological Seminary (Dr. D. James Kennedy, Chancellor). Giles was fortunate to have Dr. R.C. Sproul as an instructor for many classes.

Doug Giles is the host of ClashRadio.com, the co-founder and co-host of the Warriors & Wildmen podcast (660K downloads) and the man behind ClashDaily.com. In addition to driving ClashDaily.com (260M+ page views), Giles is the author of several #1 Amazon best-sellers including his most recent book, If Masculinity Is "Toxic", Call Jesus Radioactive.

Doug is also an artist and a filmmaker and his online gallery can be seen at DougGiles.Art. His first film, Biblical Badasses: A Raw Look at Christianity and Art, is available via DougGiles.Art.

Doug's writings have appeared on several other print and online news sources, including Townhall.com, The WashingtonTimes, The Daily Caller, Fox Nation, Human Events, USA Today, The Wall Street Journal, The Washington Examiner, American Hunter Magazine, and ABC News.

Giles and his wife Margaret have two daughters, Hannah and Regis. Hannah devastated ACORN with her 2009 nation-shaking undercover videos and she currently stars in the explosive 2018 Tribeca Documentary, Acorn and The Firestorm.

Regis has been featured in Elle, American Hunter, and Variety magazines. Regis is also the author of a powerful new book titled, How Not To Be A #Me-Too Victim, But A #WarriorChick. Regis and Hannah are both black belts in Gracie/Valente Jiu-Jitsu.

One of Doug's proudest moments came on October 11th, 2018 when Facebook banned him for life from his two million followers, because he was just too effective at reaching people with the Biblical truth and common sense.

Doug Giles

Speaking Engagements

Doug Giles speaks to college, business, community, church, advocacy and men's groups throughout the United States and internationally. His expertise includes issues of Christianity and culture, masculinity vs. wussification, God and government, big game hunting and fishing, raising righteous kids in a rank culture, the Second Amendment, personal empowerment, and social change. To invite Doug to speak at your next event, log on to DougGiles.org and fill out the invitation request.

Psalms of War

Accolades for Giles include ...

– Giles was recognized as one of "The 50 Best Conservative Columnists Of 2015"

– Giles was recognized as one of "The 50 Best Conservative Columnists Of 2014"

– Giles was recognized as one of "The 50 Best Conservative Columnists Of 2013"

– ClashDaily.com was recognized as one of "The 100 Most Popular Conservative Websites For 2013 and 2020"

– Doug was noted as "Hot Conservative New Media Superman" By Politichicks

Between 2002 – 2006, Doug's 3-minute daily commentary in Miami received seven Silver Microphone Awards and two Communicator Awards.

Doug Giles

What others say about Doug Giles

For a generation, at least, Western Society has been leveling its ideological guns on men -- that is on males, "maleness". For a good chunk of that stretch, Doug Giles -- author, hunter, commentator, broadcaster -- has taken up the cause of his fellow "dudes". His latest salvo in this desperately needed pro-XY chromosome crusade is If Masculinity Is 'Toxic', Call Jesus Radioactive. Delivered in the lively, inimitable style those familiar with Doug have come to recognize, the book confronts modern-day misandry, head on. The significance of dads, husbands, sons, brothers -- men! -- has become one of the gasping and endangered themes of our effeminized, gender-addled era. With the release of this newest tome, Doug aims to pump some life back into that foundational truth. If Masculinity Is 'Toxic', Call Jesus Radioactive tracks through the Gospel of Matthew -- a winning, easy-to-follow format -- highlighting how Jesus demonstrates what God expects of men. For all that, the book goes a long way toward sketching much of what the Creator envisions for every person -- so the ladies will benefit from perusing these pages as well.

Steve Pauwels
Editor-In-Chief, DailySurge.com

"Giles aims his arrows at the pusillanimous pastors who have bred a generation of mamby pamby Christian men who cower before the wicked. Giles challenges 'Rise up O men of God!'"

- Steven Hotze, MD
Hotze Health & Wellness Center

Psalms of War

Doug's podcast can be seen and heard at ClashRadio.com.

Doug Giles

Books by Doug Giles

If Masculinity is 'Toxic' Call Jesus Radioactive

Would Jesus Vote For Trump?

Rules For Radical Christians: 10 Biblical Disciplines for Influential Believers

Pussification: The Effeminization Of The American Male

Raising Righteous And Rowdy Girls

Raising Boys Feminists Will Hate

Rise, Kill and Eat: A Theology of Hunting From Genesis to Revelation.

If You're Going Through Hell, Keep Going

My Grandpa is a Patriotic Badass

A Coloring Book for College Cry Babies

Sandy Hook Massacre: When Seconds Count, Police Are Minutes Away

The Bulldog Attitude: Get It or ... Get Left Behind

A Time To Clash

10 Habits of Decidedly Defective People: The Successful Loser's Guide to Life

Political Twerps, Cultural Jerks, Church Quirks

Biblical Badasses: The Women

Psalms of War

In, If Masculinity Is 'Toxic', Call Jesus Radioactive, bestselling author Doug Giles offers a view of Jesus that CNN and the ladies on The View will probably not like. That said, Giles is a guessin' that his take on the 30-year-old Rebel from Galilee will be a breath of fresh air to people who're sick of postmodernism's soft focused, politically correct, pale-skinned, wussy Jesus that the enemies of the cross are foisting upon the washed and unwashed masses. Drawing heavily off the Book of Matthew, Giles's exposition of the overt masculine traits that Jesus exhibited, both in word and deed, will forever change how you see and hear The Son of Man. Many topics touched on this spicy tome have been ignored by gelded ministers beholden to their crowds' finicky palette and their purse strings, of course. In, If Masculinity Is 'Toxic', Call Jesus Radioactive, you'll see painted in Matthew's prose and Giles' wicked insight and sense of humor that Jesus Christ was anything and everything but a doe-eyed thirtysomething Mr. Rogers do-gooder. Be prepared to have your religious idols smashed and life challenged like never before as you plow through this book.

Made in the USA
Las Vegas, NV
27 January 2022